Why Are They Like That?
Lesbians

Questions you've dared to ask, answered by real people, celebrities and experts

A book series based on the award-winning sharing project that's captured worldwide attention helping people in their personal, social and business relationships

Phillip J. Milano

For Robin, Jacob, Lucas and Ben

Publisher:
Y Forum
yforum@yforum.com

ISBN: 978-1-07-951321-9

Cover and interior layout by Sandy Weber,
Key 3 Creative, Jacksonville, Florida
Cover photo credit: Rawpixel. Stock photo for illustrative purposes
only; any person depicted is a posed model.

Content based in part on the popular Y? sharing project and Dare
to Ask column

Find out more about the author, upcoming books and speeches at
www.phillipmilano.com, www.facebook.com/PhillipJMilano or
@PhillipMilano.

Books In This Series

Why Are They Like That? Blacks

Why Are They Like That? Whites

Why Are They Like That? Hispanics

Why Are They Like That? Asians

Why Are They Like That? Gay Men

Why Are They Like That? Lesbians

Why Are They Like That? Women

Why Are They Like That? Men

Why Are They Like That? Rich and Poor

Why Are They Like That? Religious (or not)

Why Are They Like That? Disabled People

Why Are They Like That? Young and Old

Praise for the Y? sharing project and the book "I Can't Believe You Asked That!" (Perigee)

"Milano is quietly revolutionizing cross-cultural communication..."
- Pulitzer Prize-winning columnist Leonard Pitts

"If you've ever hesitated to ask a question because you think it might be considered insensitive or impolitic, now is your chance ... Nothing is considered out of bounds..."
- CNN Headline News

"(It) tells more about who we are and how we feel about each other than you're likely to learn from a dozen sociology texts…"
- Washington Post News Service

"Mr. Milano has dared to open the field of debate to the maximum…"
- Le Monde, Paris

"(A) remarkable contribution to cross-cultural understanding…"
- The (London) Guardian

"A truly rare achievement … has the potential to have a profound impact on the way we all see and understand each other..."
- Playboy magazine

"It's an incredible book. It diffuses everything ... Nothing is off limits, and the questions have that childlike honesty to them..."
- Dee Snider, Twisted Sister; host, "Dee Snider Radio"

"A take-no-prisoners attitude prevails between the volume's covers . . . This book is hard to put down..."
- Midwest Book Review

"A+ (highest rating) … Everything you wanted to know but were afraid to ask gets tackled here ..."
- Entertainment Weekly

4

CONTENTS

Introduction

Why Are They Like That? is a series of books based on an award-winning worldwide sharing project in which real people, experts and celebrities talk about things that make us different from each other. Silly things. Sad things. Funny things. Profound things.

Read with an open mind and we believe that by the time you're finished you'll have a much better understanding of how to make more and real friends, money and love. It's that simple.

Why? Because this isn't about trying to get ahead with diversity training. We are well beyond that. According to the Census Bureau, by 2050 the United States will have no racial or ethnic minority.

No, this is about moving past talking about how to understand each other to talking to each other. Right now.

That's why there's no agenda to these books other than getting the conversation going. We can discuss studies and methods for elevating social consciousness all we want, but there is no substitute for real dialogue.

That's where Why Are They Like That? stands apart from other books on the topic. You will see how people talk about their real differences of race, religion, sex, disability and more.

The success of the approach is proven: It's based on the ground-breaking Y? website project, blog and column that have attracted millions of visitors and worldwide media attention.

Our hope is that by reading, you will become more comfortable asking and answering the questions yourself, expecting the unexpected in return and helping change the ground rules for how we learn from and about each other. To that end, we wrap up each book in the series with our O.U.T.L.O.U.D. Method for Dialogue, with tips to help you get your own conversations started. Ultimately, that is what this effort is all about.

After all, if you want to make more friends, money and love, you better know the people you're talking to, selling to or opening to. Knowledge isn't just power. It's all power.

Enjoy.

Phillip J. Milano
Founder, Y?

Is it just all about sex for lesbians?

They asked:

My wife is in her 40s and until recently was never approached by lesbians in her workplace. They know she is married with a family, but now they are relentless in pursuing her sexually (she thinks it is rather exciting to be noticed). Not only are extramarital affairs wrong, but breaking up a family for your own ends is even worse. Is the lesbian community all about sex only?

Jack, 41, Lubbock, Texas

You said:

As a rule, no. Yeah, we like sex, but usually it's about the emotional aspect. This is one of the reasons homosexuality makes more sense to me than straight sex. Women know what women like, and men know what men like.

Dwanny, 51, lesbian, Springtown, Texas

You cannot judge a whole group of people by what some in that group do. My husband has been hit on by black women, white women, younger women and older women. But I still can't conclude that all women are that way. However, sexual harassment by anyone (lesbian or otherwise) at work is against the law, and your wife needs to report it. Work is no place to be sexually pursued relentlessly.

M.G., 30, female, Jacksonville

Lesbians as a group are just like any other group: full of many different people with very different attitudes. If your wife is encountering a lesbian who seems overly interested in sex, I would attribute her behavior only to her as a person, not to all lesbians in general.

Amy, 20, bisexual, College Park, Md.

We found:

Catch the "she thinks it is rather exciting to be noticed" part of Jack's question?

So did Suzanne Westenhoefer, a self-described "femmy lezzie" comedian (whether she could pass for a hot soccer mom in the school parent pickup line is entirely up to you — visit suzannew.com).

"I think his wife's encouraging this to get attention from hubby," said Westenhoefer, the first out lesbian comic to appear on David Letterman's show and to have her own HBO special.

Beyond that, she thinks Jack is kind of a jerk, although she used a different word.

"He's taking a giant leap from 'a woman is coming on to my wife' to 'all lezzies are evil.' I mean, Pat Robertson doesn't make leaps that quickly."

Jack should be more concerned with making sure his wife's harassers are reported than generalizing about lesbian carnal preoccupation, Westenhoefer said.

Why some people make these kinds of broad assumptions may be driven by the fact that sexual orientation is the main thing differentiating gay people from straight people, she said. "So if that's the only thing you know about a gay person, you might hyper-focus on it."

Sure, some gay women pursue straight women, but to Westenhoefer, they are often "tragic lesbians" who aren't consciously going after straights but instead are engaging in self-punishment. "It's the lesbian-who-can-never-fall-in-love-with-a-woman-who's-available thing. Yeah, I've seen that."

How to come out and not get shut out

They asked:

I am bisexual. I want to come out completely, as I am sick of pretending to be someone I am not. But I'm leery of coming out to specific people. For example, my father's side of the family is very conservative. My relationship with each of them is fragile enough that I believe if I come out, they will cease to love me.

A.E., bisexual female, Ohio

You said:

If they can't accept you for who you are, you shouldn't waste your time trying to get them to love you.

Norbert, 17, bisexual, Minn.

Please think about this. One thing about being in this type of lifestyle is that you open yourself up to all types of disease and emotional turmoil. There are some long-term effects that aren't really good. Women were not designed to be with other women. I speak from experience. Trust me, it isn't worth it.

T.M., Raleigh, N.C.

If you live where people are not accepting of this, be careful, as there may be safety concerns. However, if you're in a more liberal environment, it is an overwhelming relief to do so. You are not opening yourself up to disease or long-term harm by coming out. You are more likely to suffer more in the long-term by "hiding in the closet" because of constant fear, pressure and shame.

Jason, 29, gay, New York

Most of my gay friends came out only to find that their families already knew or suspected.

Dot, Los Angeles

We found:

Come out, come out, wherever you are?

You might want to do a little recon work first — and, by all means, make sure you're doing it for you and no one else.

So says Candace Gingrich, Youth & Campus Engagement associate director for the Human Rights Campaign. "It's good to test the waters first. Maybe before you come out to a parent, talk to a favorite uncle or aunt who's supportive and will be a friendly ear."

Gingrich, a lesbian and author of the autobiography "The Accidental Activist,", knows what it's like to come out, publicly and really publicly. In 1987, she told her own family. Then, in 1994, she clued in pretty much all six inhabitable continents, taking on half-brother Newt Gingrich in the media for his anti-gay views when he became Speaker of the House.

For most people, "Coming out to family still remains one of the more frightening things to do, and it requires patience. We want them to say, 'I love you just as you are' . . . but we often forget parents and family members may need time to get used to it."

Gingrich recommended consulting local gay advocacy groups or the Internet, such as sites like hrc.org, for more advice on coming out.

Oh, and timing can be everything.

"Find the right situation to perhaps say 'Mom and Dad, I want to talk to you because I recently realized something about myself, and you are too important for me to not be my true self with you," she said.

"That approach may be more successful than just doing it at Thanksgiving dinner. 'Pass the salt, Mom and Dad, I'm gay' is not the wisest thing to do."

Having fun with sex … and this L-word

They asked:

Is it true that Libyans have less sects than any other combination and eventually stop having sects altogether?

Jeremiah C., Burney, California

You said:

Not the Libyans I know. Sounds suspiciously like a little piece of hetero male ego-salving mythology to me — i.e. "Oh, those Libyans are frigid anyway, so it doesn't matter that they don't want me."

Ann, 38, straight, Kansas City, Mo.

I have yet to meet a Libyan couple who isn't into sects. I think that's based on the stereotype that women don't like a lot of sects and men do, which isn't necessarily true.

Jack, 21, gray male, Oshkosh, Wis.

There have been studies done that show that of Libyans surveyed after 10 years in a relationship, only 1 percent of them have sects at least three times a week. Keep in mind, definitions of sects are mutable according to the individual, and it was only having sects three or more times. Who's to say that having sects only two times a week isn't satisfying to a couple?

Nicole, 21, State College, Penn.

Many Libyans have more sects because their partners know how to please them and don't need recovery time between organisms.

Dina M., bisectual, Chicago

We found:

Can you imagine how incredibly goofy we'd sound if we changed just a few strategic words in our reply? But we would never pander to anyone who gets nervous reading certain words.

To answer Jeremiah's query, there's conflicting (and oddly worded) research on Libyans and the frequency and quality of their sects.

For example, researchers Philip Blumstein and Pepper Schwartz in their 1983 book "American Couples" said Libyans had quite a bit less sects than straight or gray male couples — only one in three Libyans had sects at least once a week. Consequently, "Libyan Bed Death" became a popular phrase.

Conjecture was that this was because of things like "internalized homophobia" and "hyper-female" behavior (females have a decreased sects drive as they age, other surveys show).

Critics said the study may have focused on the quantity and not quality of Libyan sects. For example, Libyans more often associate love with their sects, spend more time when having sects, have more frequent organisms and have choral sects more often, according to some surveys, including one — "Sectual Function in Libyans and Libyan Relationships" by the New Jersey-based Institute for Personal Growth (ipgcounseling.com), which provides counseling and health care to Libyans and others.

Looked at that way, Libyans may not have sects as often, but may have "healthier" sects than straight couples, sects therapist Suzanne Iasenza has theorized.

However, if we're just talking about flat-out "regular" sects done the old-fashioned way, it may be true the Libyans have slightly less. The IPG Counseling survey did find that Libyans overall have sects about once or twice a month, compared to about once a week for non-Libyan women.

Do gays feel they are still being shunned?

They asked:

Do people of the homosexual preference feel they are shunned?

Karissa, Elizabethton, Tenn.

You said:

Being gay isn't a preference, it's a reality. It also doesn't help that many groups call LGBT people "perverts" and lie about them. It is definitely true that LGBT people feel shunned.

Erin, 18, bisexual, Illinois

Yes, and occasionally they are murdered ... and I imagine being murdered might make a person feel shunned.

Carrie, 21, bisexual, Houston

It's not fair when I take my partner out for a dinner and have to avert my eyes from those casting a scornful look.

Alaina, 28, lesbian, Cincinnati

I am tired of being the token lesbian at work. Of being left out of family reunions so "Aunt Judy and Uncle Joe" won't feel uncomfortable. I want the right to see my spouse in the hospital. My friend wanted the right to be called when her lover was killed in Iraq. The military called her parents instead. They had been a couple for 10 years. I want to lead my son's Cub Scout den without being undercover.

Kara, 51, lesbian, Austin

We found:

Some numbers: A Human Rights Campaign workplace survey of Lesbian, Gay, Bisexual and Transgender (LGBT) people found that 51 percent hide their LGBT identity, fewer than half feel OK talking about sex or relationships with co-workers, nearly six of 10 hear derogatory comments about LGBT people, 42 percent feel they must lie about their personal life, half of those who aren't open don't reveal their identity because they feel it'll bother others, 40 percent say others get uncomfortable if they mention their partner and some say they're ignored by co-workers after revealing their identity.

Yet, "in general, things are getting better — though they're nowhere near where they should be," said HRC spokesman and Huffington Post blogger Michael Cole-Schwartz. "People getting annoyed because you put a picture of your partner on your desk happens less because it's becoming less of an oddity."

One problem is that LGBT people often grow up shunning their own reality, and then get hit with so much that reminds them they are different that it reinforces feeling ostracized, he said.

"Just last night, the concierge in my building tells me there was a message for my 'roommate' — well, clearly we're a couple, and that can be off-putting when it's not recognized."

The best thing to do: Learn about LGBT people's lives, Cole-Schwartz said.

"Invite someone gay to dinner ... not because they're gay, but because you want to get to know them. Some straight people latch on to 'that gay person' as their token diverse person; it's like, 'Oh, let's see what the gay person thinks.' "

But if you do want to ask something, maybe see how they feel about the fact that in too many states, it's still legal to fire them just because they're gay.

Just don't ask it at the water cooler.

No love lost between lesbians and gay men?

They asked:

Why do some queens hate lesbians? You would think we would support each other.

Imari, 47, lesbian, Austin, Texas

You said:

Because most queens care about one thing: themselves. They don't like straight people, they don't like bisexuals and they certainly don't like lesbians. . . . They are a main reason the gay community has a hard time organizing.

Alaina, 28, lesbian, Cincinnati

Some gay men (I assume by "queen" you mean "gay men") are uncomfortable with lesbians for the same reasons men in general are uncomfortable with women. And in addition to general cultural differences, gay men have no sexual motivation for interacting (civilly) with women. Thus, sometimes the lack of understanding or tolerance between them.

David, Los Angeles

Sadly, I think a lack of understanding causes some queens or lesbians to dislike or suspect each other. The Queer/LGBT community does not hold a monopoly on tolerance, and some members are as bad as the homophobic/heterosexist people they complain about.

Kaye, 26, lesbian, Hammond, La.

Gay males, or "queens" as you so eloquently put it, do not have an irrational hate of lesbians. Many people asked that question after seeing the popular NBC show Will and Grace, when Jack had an irrational dislike toward lesbians. This is not realistic behavior when referring to the gay community. Usually we stick together.

Kevin, 19, gay, Downey, Calif.

We found:

Sure, some gays and lesbians aren't pals, said Kathy Belge (kathybelge.com), Dipstick half of the lesbian writing duo Lipstick & Dipstick, who pen a gay advice column.

"It's rooted in sexism, classism and some homophobia — not wanting to see the flaming queen, or not accepting the butch lesbian," said Belge, who co-wrote "Lipstick & Dipstick's Essential Guide to Lesbian Relationships." "Personally I think that's bull."

Another issue that might cause some lesbians some ill will has to do with the AIDS crisis, she said.

"Lesbians were the main caregivers of gay men during the '80s and '90s, and some don't think they've seen gay men coming out for lesbian causes the way lesbians rallied around gay men."

Overall, though, Belge doesn't buy into the broad stereotype of gay/lesbian friction.

"I have a lot of close, great gay male friends . . . we come together over gay marriage, gay youth causes and more.

"The bottom line is, we have more in common than not . . . Sure, a gay man can be bitchy, and so can some lesbians. Just because they are that way with a particular person doesn't mean they don't like lesbians."

If you get hot and bothered over girls, and you're a girl, too...

They asked:

I met this girl a few days ago who is absolutely gorgeous and has an awesome personality. I feel I'm sexually attracted to her, which is creeping me out a lot. I also have some lesbian fantasies. Am I bi?

Ashley, 16, New York

You said:

Welcome to my world.

Keith, bisexual, Dallas

You're SIXTEEN. At your age, going through a car wash might turn you on.

Ann, 38, straight, Kansas City, Mo.

You are bi-curious.

Freda, 25, bisexual, Indianola, Miss.

Turned on by girls and lesbian fantasies? I'd say you're bi.

Amy, 23, straight, Louisiana

I am the exact same way. I was weirded out myself. I don't think you're bi until you act on it.

Tiffany, 20, Detroit

Sexuality tends to occur on a sliding scale.

Laura, 20, bisexual, Grand Rapids, Mich,

I feel the same as you as far as feeling ashamed. I come from a Christian background. I'm "sick," "perverted" or, as some call it, "demon-possessed." One can see how I want to be restored back to my religion and to God but at the same time feel alienated and rejected by both.

Anonymous, Daytona Beach

It means you are in a very experimental stage.

Natasha, 25, straight, Marion, Ark.

It might just be a phase. I had that phase, too.

A.M., 17, straight, Des Moines, Iowa

We found:

We debated which of two definitions of bisexuality to use, but in the end decided to go both ways.

One definition stresses potential: People with the capacity to be attracted to more than one gender might be considered bisexual, even if they never act on it, said Loraine Hutchins, Ph.D. (lorainehutchins.com), a sex educator who co-edited the seminal book "Bi Any Other Name: Bisexual People Speak Out."

On that score, a National Center for Health Statistics survey found 5.6 percent of males and 12.9 percent of females ages 18 to 44 said they were attracted to both males and females.

The other definition looks at people who self-identify as "bisexual" and act on it. The same National Center for Health Statistics survey found 1.8 percent of men and 2.8 percent of women ages 18 to 44 identified as bisexual.

And, while some studies now indicate bisexuality isn't a "phase" but is a lifetime identity, it doesn't mean all teen girls who are feeling attraction to both males and females are bi, Hutchins said.

"It's easier for girls in our society to experiment. . . . But this girl has all the time in the world and doesn't have to 'declare,' like it's a college major," she said. "She should check out where the scared feelings are coming from . . . perhaps at a Gay-Straight Alliance at her high school. It could mean a lot of different things. The first time I had an erotic dream about another woman I was repulsed . . . but then I had other experiences that were more positive."

Where do lesbians go to see strippers?

They asked:

Do lesbians go to strip clubs? Or is the idea of stripping and dancing for money offensive?

Annie, 38, Tucson, Ariz.

You said:

I wish there were lesbian strip clubs. That would be an ideal environment. We have to settle for "gentleman's clubs." And I find the old men creepy.

Rebecca, 26, lesbian, Kansas City, Kan.

I've been to gentleman's clubs before. I found it more fun than arousing. Yes, there are some gay women who are highly offended by the objectification of women for money, but I think it is more a feminist issue than a gay/straight one.

Kæreste, 22, lesbian, Jacksonville

I know a lot of lesbians who find it offensive, but I also know a lot who find it plain old hot! We're not all crazy feminists.

Melissa, 25, Calgary, Alberta

There are strip clubs that cater to lesbians (you might remember Ben Affleck "accidently" went to one in Canada).

Candy, Atlanta

Many strip clubs don't permit women customers in. It'd be like letting a Lexus salesman hang out in a Mercedes dealership.

David, 47, Knoxville, Tenn.

We found:

Marketing sex to women, gay or not, can be, well, a little complicated.

Take pornographic magazines geared toward lesbians. It can be difficult to make a go of it when a large chunk of your demographic finds the very idea repugnant, the editor-in-chief of On Our Backs told us a few years ago. The magazine has since folded.

Erotic dancing is no different. A segment of the lesbian community condemns it, says Lillian Faderman (lillianfaderman.net), a former Fresno State historian, lesbian and former stripper (we hit the trifecta with that one).

"Lesbian strip clubs have come and gone since the '80s," said Faderman, author of the acclaimed "Odd Girls and Twilight Lovers" (Penguin). "One person I interviewed who opened one said lesbians are shy about participating in something like that that is so open, and publicly sexual."

Such clubs have met with protests. Tel Aviv's now-closed Minerva Club was picketed by feminists who denounced its lesbian striptease shows as exploitative.

Faderman says things have opened up since the days she took it all off in the 1950s and '60s, when owners of underground gay nightclubs even shined flashlights between same-sex patrons on the dance floor to make sure they weren't touching.

Nowadays, more lesbians feel they have every right to enjoy erotic dancers as a liberating way to boldly claim their sexuality.

And just to clear up any false notions, there's no big mystery about what goes into a strip act for lesbians, Faderman added.

"I don't like to generalize that women aren't aroused by visual things — but from what I gather, acts in these clubs these days would likely be less graphic than a lap dance, but yes, they do strip, and it's very similar to regular stripping."

Is it just harder to be gay?

They asked:

What is the hardest thing to deal with as a gay individual?

C.D., Johnson City, Tenn.

You said:

Probably the sudden death of a loved one. However, many people have a misconception that being gay is all we are. I'm sure straight people don't dwell on their heterosexuality ("Do these pants make me look straight?"; "I wonder if people at work know I'm straight?"; "Wow, she's hot! I wonder if she's straight?"). I believe people who think we lead exotic, secret gay lives don't think they know any of us. We're standing right in front of you. We go to work, mow the lawn, take the kids to soccer, throw in a load of laundry and sleep in on Saturdays. We are exactly like you.

FreedaBee, 42, lesbian, Orange County, Calif.

The hardest thing to deal with is how little people know. I still come across people who think I chose my orientation, and it infuriates me.

Jordan, 15, gay, Jacksonville

Not being able to walk down the street hand in hand with my girlfriend, the love of my life, without getting the glares, hearing the whispers and getting the occasional comments. I would love to be able to give my girlfriend a gentle kiss while we are in a store or parking lot, but people look at us like we have lobsters crawling out of our ears.

Mary, 25, lesbian, Springfield, Vt.

We found:

Being gay? Not a problem, says Angelo Pezzote, a New York author and psychotherapist who's worked with hundreds of gay men and women and runs doctorangelo.com.

Being OK with being gay? Different story.

"The hardest thing overall for gay people that I treat, those with substance abuse, safe sex, relationship or anxiety problems, is self-acceptance. The shame that comes from the 'gay stigma' — that gay men are not real men, for example — causes a sense of shame."

Those who don't address the issue set themselves up for lower self-esteem, amid all of life's other struggles, sometimes triggering symptoms such as depression or alcohol abuse, he said.

"The issue of 'immorality' gets drilled into us in the overall culture," said Pezzote, who is gay. "And the issue becomes 'Am I lovable the way I am?' "

For those gays beyond such issues, he said, the daily challenge often boils down to whether to mute their orientation and behaviors in public to avoid sneers, or losing a job, or even violent reactions — especially when a good chunk of Americans still believe being gay is unacceptable.

Pezzote said some even feel pressure to show others they adhere to societal "norms." He used as an example Lance Bass of 'N Sync, who came out but told People magazine he was a "straight-acting gay" — a "typical guy" who loved to "watch football and drink beer."

"Whenever we tone down part of who we are to be more acceptable, to conform, we are stamping out a part of us," Pezzote said. "We just need to be who we are: people who are gay."

Is 'Born this Way' just a Lady Gaga song?

They asked:

Could sexual orientation be genetically pushed by excessive male or female hormones during pregnancy?

Rod, 50, straight, Jacksonville

You said:

It could be hormonal, but we've had homosexual people around since history began to be written down and kept track of. There are also gay animal groups that don't eat anything in order to alter their hormones. It could be an in-utero hormonal issue, but not one caused by the pill (or only by the pill). . . . I also read about a study that said hormones produced during pregnancy could cause homosexuality if there is too much or too little. The study was on humans, but the experimenting was on rats.

Dina Marie, 19, bisexual, Chicago

The theory for gay men is that male fetuses who develop in the presence of higher-than-average levels of male hormones like androgen are more likely to be gay. They are, in a sense "hyper-masculine."

Gordon, Salt Lake City, Utah

If that were the case, then the population of gays should have skyrocketed after the pill was introduced given the number of women who used the pill. Also, it wouldn't explain why there were gays before the pill was introduced or explain why there are gays like me who are children of good Catholic parents who didn't use birth control pills.

Shelly, 49, bisexual, Pennsylvania

No. Not sure what else to say. What, did your preacher use that line to justify his Neanderthal stance on birth control or something?

Ann, 38, straight, Kansas City, Mo.

We found:

In recent years, researchers have found evidence that points to biological contributors to sexual orientation:

— Men who have several older biological brothers are a bit more likely to be gay than men who don't, according to a study Proceedings of the National Academy of Sciences by human sexuality researcher Anthony F. Bogaert of Brock University in Canada. It could be because the boys' mom develops some type of immune response to succeeding male fetuses, though another theory is that the youngest brother might get exposed to more androgens like testosterone while in the womb.

— Men's index fingers are generally shorter than their ring fingers, while women's are usually about the same length. This likely has to do with higher testosterone levels in males, which affects the length of their extremities in different ways (keep this in mind as you read further down). But lesbians' index fingers also tend to be shorter than their ring fingers — unlike straight women — and that may mean lesbians are hit with more prenatal androgens, too, according to research by Michigan State University neuroscience professor Marc Breedlove and colleagues.

A different study found that gay men's index fingers are a lot shorter than their ring fingers — even shorter than straight men's, write researchers Glenn Wilson and Qazi Rahman in "Born Gay." Again, "more prenatal testosterone" might be at work.

— Testosterone in the womb may affect another extremity in men. Penises averaged about 1/3 inch longer in gay men (6.32 inches) than straight men, researcher Bogaert found, when he and Scott Hershberger of California State University-Long Beach looked at the Kinsey Report's 1938-1963 data.

Scientists don't know why there's a difference, but according to an article in the Los Angeles Times, some speculate that gay men might be exposed to more testosterone early on in the womb, leading to an enhanced penis, but then they receive lower levels later in the womb, possibly causing more feminine characteristics such as attraction to men.

Two straight guys walk into a gay bar...

They asked:

Is it rude to go to a gay bar if you are not gay?

Molli, Sioux City, Iowa

You said:

I have no problem with women coming to women's bars (duh). My problem is when they come with men, dance with men and smooch with men in lesbian bars. It would be nice if there was one little piece of the world where who I am and what I do is the norm.

Marianne, 54, lesbian, Portland, Ore.

I've gone on a number of occasions with an openly gay friend. We like to dance. I celebrated my 30th birthday with good-looking men who didn't want to sleep with me, but who were very glad to spin me around the dance floor. As long as you tip waitstaff well and aren't judgmental, there shouldn't be a problem.

Cari, Galveston, Texas

It is absolutely OK for straights to go to gay bars as long as they aren't rude or hateful. Keep in mind you may be hit on by someone of your gender. After all, it is a gay bar. If you respectfully tell someone you are straight, they will almost always back off and go flirt with someone they may actually be able to pick up.

Kaye, 26, lesbian, Hammond, La.

We found:

Some words from the wise playwright Meryl Cohn, who penned the longtime-syndicated "Ms. Behavior" gay etiquette column and is author of "Do What I Say: Ms. Behavior's Guide to Gay and Lesbian Etiquette."

26

— First, it's fine to go. "Sometimes straight women want to go to a gay male bar or a lesbian bar, just so they can dance or hang with their friends without being hit on."

— But don't gawk or harass. "Years ago, at this dyke bar a friend owned, they used to have men who'd come and want to get in, just to look at lesbians. I'd like to think things are different than they used to be."

— And don't fake it. "You don't have to pretend to be gay to fit in, or pretend to be interested in someone so that you'll 'pass' for gay. If you want to blend in [and are a straight male], you don't have to make out with a man to do so. In general, the etiquette is the same as it is anywhere: Don't do something to make someone uncomfortable."

— News flash! People may not think you're straight. "Don't be offended if somebody assumes you are gay if you're in a gay bar . . . in other words, don't hang out in a gay bar and then punch someone in the face if they ask you to dance."

— Realize not all gay bars are alike. "It's true the music has traditionally been better in gay bars, and the fashion and grooming for many men is definitely better in gay bars. But some have beautiful decor, and some are just bar bars like an old man's bar . . . some even are for big, hairy men who are called bears, some are for lipstick lesbians, some are for sport lesbians . . .

"My brother is gay, and I asked him where he met his partner, and he said in a gay sports bar. I bet not a lot of people even realize there are sports bars for gays. I said [jokingly], 'Well, were they watching ice skating?' He said, 'Nope. Football.' "

Why follow the Bible chapter and verse on homosexuality?

They asked:

Why do fundamentalist Christians cite the Old Testament for their views on homosexuality when it is not part of the Ten Commandments? If they follow this part of the Old Testament, how about all the other stuff in there, such as dietary restrictions?

Claire, 23, secular humanist, Los Angeles

You said:

Because it doesn't fit their larger world view of "man-and-woman" morality. The New Testament is pretty silent on the issue.

Jacob, 30, Catholic male, Sherman, Texas

Fundamentalist Christians (I am one) can be mean-spirited regarding homosexuality. We do need to make some changes. But it's erroneous to think homosexuality is only addressed in the Old Testament. The King James Version states that the "effeminate" will not enter the Kingdom of Heaven. As a Christian who has befriended some wonderful gay people, this saddens me. But I didn't write the book, nor can I change it.

Friendly Inquirer, Christian, Jacksonville

We found:

Melissa Fryrear, former gender issues analyst for the conservative Colorado Springs-based Focus on the Family and now Women's Ministry Shepherd at Heights Church in Arizona, distinguishes between the Old Testament's ceremonial laws, abolished in the New Testament, and its moral laws, reinforced in the New Testament.

"Differentiating between these two types of laws answers the question," said Fryrear, who identifies now as a single Christian and spoke with us before her departure from Focus on the Family. "Also, disobedience to ceremonial laws resulted in uncleanliness, as in Leviticus 11:24, while disobedience to moral law resulted in death, as in Leviticus 20. So there's more gravity there."

Fryrear, who turned away from life as a lesbian in 1992 after "a lot of soul-searching," said that while some biblical scholars say Jesus' silence on the matter means he did not feel it a major issue, "Jesus also did not address incest, but we would not conclude that his silence ... means that we are no longer bound to the Old Testament prohibitions in this area."

Other scholars argue homosexuality isn't a big biblical deal. Debra Haffner, past president of the progressive Sexuality Information and Education Council of the United States, pointed out in a research paper that the topic is only brought up in Leviticus 18:22 and 20:13, and Romans 1:26 and 1:27.

"The fact that only four verses explicitly address this issue implies that this subject was of relatively little importance to the authors," she writes.

Anyway, there are 17 verses alone in Leviticus on how to make a grain offering, she reminds, and plenty more condemnations on things such as eating fat and touching a menstruating woman's bedding.

Care to ratchet up the debate? Some Bible passages acknowledge sexual contact and love between men, she notes: Genesis 24:2, 2 Samuel 1:26, 1 Samuel 18:1 and 1 Samuel 19:1.

The O.U.T.L.O.U.D.
Method to Dialogue

OPEN UP: This is mostly about opening up to yourself. Why do you want to engage someone? Is it for the right reasons? The answers might help you figure out how to approach another person. A friend once told me the real reason I started Y? wasn't for me to learn more about "Buddhists in Asia or lesbians in San Francisco," but because I wanted to learn something more about myself. He was right. Acknowledging that has helped give me perspective when considering others' answers.

USE YOUR HEAD: Plan for the right question. Not all questions need to be the "wet dogs" variety. Stereotypes and clichés don't work as well as sincere attempts to talk.

TIME IT RIGHT: Create the "O.U.T.L.O.U.D. Moment". Pick your spots for provocative dialogue. Find a genuine opening rather than create a false one. It's often during those down times between all the "vital" discourse that we can most easily find a direct path to someone's point of view. If you spend enough time sitting in the cubicle next to someone of a different culture, chances are there'll come a time — over food, perhaps, or during a power outage — when the topic you've been dying to broach will wend its way naturally into the discussion.

LOCK IN ON THE TARGET: Keeping things simple can give the best chance for getting another's trust and a meaningful reply. Some of the best questions at Y?, those that prompt the most telling answers, are also often the easiest to digest. Remember, it's not about winning your point. It's what comes from the heart that counts most — and captures people's interest. Talking from the heart also means easing into things by letting someone know *why* it would help you to learn the answer to your question before you ask it.

OWN UP TO ASSUMPTIONS: One of the most refreshing and repetitive surprises of the Y? project is the difficulty in predicting how a person will respond to a question. Blacks do not think in lockstep. Nor do whites. Nor Christians or Muslims. Nor gays or straights. Be receptive to another's ideas. Wipe the slate clean and listen to the content of the message, not the color or culture of the messenger.

UNLOAD YOUR EXPECTATIONS: Many of us are thinner-skinned than we'll admit. When we get hit with an answer or comment we hadn't anticipated, our emotions can often get caught off-balance, and our egos get bruised. The solution: Expect the unexpected. You'll never be blindsided or taken aback by information that doesn't gibe with your worldview.

DIGEST THE DIALOGUE: Learning about others doesn't stop when the talking's over. Assess what you're told and how it fits with or departs from your perspectives. Recap your discussion with a third party to distill the most relevant information into its most meaningful points.

ABOUT THE AUTHOR

Phillip J. Milano is the founder of Y? The National Forum on People's Differences, the acclaimed cross-cultural dialogue project that encourages people to ask unflinching, politically incorrect questions about our differences.

Since its creation in 1998, Phillip's web site, YForum.com, has attracted millions of visitors and thousands of questions and answers. He has been featured on CBS, CNN, BET and the BBC, and in numerous newspapers, including The Washington Post, New York Times and USA Today.

He is the author of the Perigee book "I Can't Believe You Asked That!" as well as writer of the pioneering newspaper column/blog "Dare to Ask."

Mr. Milano is a 25-year newspaper veteran. He received his Master of Business Administration from Northern Illinois University and his Bachelor of Science in Journalism from Southern Illinois University.

SPEECHES AND APPEARANCES

Mr. Milano is an in-demand speaker. For bookings, contact

Contemporary Issues Agency
809 Turnberry Drive, Waunakee, WI 53597-2256
Phone: 800-843-2179
Fax: 608-849-6311
www.CIAspeakers.com
Info@CIAspeakers.com